# WHERE ARE WE HEADED?

Guidelines for the
Catholic Charismatic Renewal

**BOOK TWO OF THE SERVANT SERIES**

STEPHEN CLARK

**PUBLISHED BY
CHARISMATIC RENEWAL SERVICES, INC.**

Published by:

   Charismatic Renewal Services, Inc.

   P.O. Drawer A

   Notre Dame, Indiana 46556

Pamphlet design by Unfolding His Word

# PREFACE

This pamphlet is written primarily for leaders in the Catholic charismatic renewal. It is intended to be of help to them in making pastoral decisions regarding the development of the groups that they are responsible for. Its usefulness, however, should not be limited only to leaders in the Catholic charismatic renewal; it can be valuable reading for leaders in the charismatic renewal outside the Catholic Church. Most of the wisdom we have gained in developing a movement within the Catholic Church is helpful to groups trying to do the same thing in other churches. The pamphlet can also be valuable for leaders of the Catholic Church, and other churches, who are not involved in the charismatic renewal; it can provide an "inside view" of what the charismatic renewal is and could become. It can also show them how the charismatic renewal could become better integrated into the life of the church. Finally, it can be valuable reading for participants in the Catholic charismatic renewal (and the charismatic renewal in other churches) who do not have leadership responsibilities for the groups they are part of. We all need to see whatever vision we can of where we are headed, so that we can participate more effectively as active, responsible members.

Any leadership responsibility is a service of love. We should be willing to lay aside all self-seeking, and in humility seek the glory of God and the good of his people (Phil. 2:3-4). May he be praised.

# INTRODUCTION

At the time these guidelines are being written (1973) the charismatic renewal in the Catholic Church has emerged as one of the most vital occurrences in contemporary Christianity. It is growing more rapidly than anyone knows: the attendance at the annual international conference alone more than doubles each year. It is spreading all over the world.

Throughout Europe, Asia, Latin America and Africa, "Catholic Pentecostal" groups already exist in the midst of widespread interest. In all parts of the church and among all types of people the movement has been met with sincere interest and openness, and the hierarchy of the church has been remarkably receptive.

There are many other indications of the current success of the charismatic renewal in the Catholic Church. Catholic book publishers, for instance, are eager to acquire "Pentecostal" titles, confident that "Pentecostal" books will be successful sellers. More and more Catholic conferences and conventions are willing to hold workshops on the charismatic renewal. The movement is receiving greater coverage from the media, with newsmen like the religion editor of the **New York Times** calling it (together with the Jesus People movement) "the most vital movement in American religion today."

There is no question but that this movement has become something of extraordinary significance. If those of us who have a leadership responsibility for the charismatic renewal want "worldly success", we have it. In a day when Christian groups seem lifeless and ineffective, the renewal we are part of is alive, increasingly successful, and even gaining acceptance and respect.

If, however, those of us who have leadership responsibility for the charismatic renewal want to serve the Lord and be at the disposal of his purposes, this success should call us all the more to seek the Lord for direction. God is clearly doing something significant. He is pouring out his Spirit in a powerful way and touching the lives of hundreds of thousands. It is therefore all the more urgent for us to place ourselves at the disposal of what he is doing and to seek to further his plans and not our own. To get "worldly success" without "spiritual success" would be to build with hay and stubble (I Cor. 3:12).

What follows is a set of suggested guidelines for placing ourselves at the disposal of what the Lord is doing. Behind these guidelines lies an attempt to discern what the Lord is doing, an attempt to gain some kind of vision of what the Lord is moving towards at this moment in history. Guidelines such as these are meant to help us set a clearer and surer course of action in our service of the Lord.

# THE LONG RANGE: THE RENEWAL OF CHRISTIAN LIFE

A guiding vision can help us to make better choices, to take the right path with greater confidence. The Lord often wants to give such a vision to his people, as he did in the second half of Isaiah and the book of Revelation. The first five guidelines in this pamphlet are based on and express something of a guiding vision for the charismatic renewal today. The next six guidelines are more concerned with what we are to do in the present situation. The four guidelines after that are concerned with special problem areas that could cause us to fall short in reaching the fullness of what God may be calling us to.

**1. Our goal should not be to have a Catholic Pentecostal movement, but to have a complete renewal of Christian life in the power of the Spirit.**

There does not seem to be much question of "stopping" the charismatic renewal in the Catholic Church. The Lord is doing something and those who have been given leadership responsibility are in no position to "stop" what is happening. But we do have an influence on how the charismatic renewal develops. God always works in history through men, and the decisions and actions of those men can serve what he is doing or be a hindrance he has to work around.

At the moment, we are faced with decisions that must be made concerning the future form of the Catholic charismatic renewal. Should this work of the Lord become a specialized movement in the Catholic Church? Should it take the form of a sectarian movement? Should it coalesce with similar movements in other churches? Should it become something like a religious order or secular institute? In these areas our decisions have consequences for the Lord's work, and we very much need his guidance.

What is the Lord doing? What is the Lord's plan? Anyone who tries to give a complete description of what the Lord is doing or who expects to fully understand his plan is sure to go astray. He said in Isaiah 55:

For my thoughts are not your thoughts, neither are your ways my ways, says the Lord.

For as the heavens are higher than the earth, so are my ways higher than your ways and my thoughts than your thoughts.

We cannot expect to comprehend fully what the Lord is doing, and yet the Lord does expect us to read "the signs of the times" (Mt. 16:1-4) and to understand in some way what his plan is.

There are many ways of coming to an understanding of what the Lord is about and of what he wants us to do. In the charismatic renewal we have been given the gift of prophecy, so that the Lord can speak to us directly, and the gift of wisdom, so that he can lead us into a deeper understanding of what he would see happen. Some of that prophecy has directed and confirmed what is being written here; some of that wisdom has made parts of these pages possible. But there is another way of getting an insight into what the Lord is doing, and it is that way that I want to look into here.

Once when our original group in Ann Arbor wanted to know what to do in our own local situation, we set aside a day to listen to the Lord and find his direction. His message to us was that we should not make plans according to our own good ideas, but that we should look to what he is doing and put ourselves at the disposal of that. Since then, that word from the Lord has often proved itself to be a valuable guide in following the Lord. We should try to discern what he is doing and serve that.

There are some things which are clearly objectives that the Lord is trying to accomplish. These can be guides to our direction:

1) spiritual renewal: the most striking aspect of the charismatic renewal is the recovery of the power of the Spirit to live the Christian life in today's world. Whatever the Lord is trying to do through the charismatic renewal, spiritual renewal is certainly a primary goal.

2) new patterns of life: the charismatic renewal has so far been a creative source for new patterns of coming together and living as Christians. The emergence of new life patterns is a clear thrust of the charismatic renewal.

3) renewal of the Catholic Church: it does not seem accidental that the charismatic renewal within the Catholic Church (the Catholic Pentecostal Movement) has assumed a place of special importance within the whole Pentecostal Movement, with a significant effect on the growth and development of the movement among other Christians.

4) the unity of Christians: from the very beginning the movement within the Catholic Church has had an ecumenical dimension that has brought Catholics into a spiritual unity with many other Christians. In fact, many of the groups that are involved in the Catholic charismatic renewal have many members who do not belong to the Roman Catholic Church.

These four developments are clearly occurring within the charismatic renewal in the Catholic

Church today, and they seem to be happening as a direct response to God's Spirit. They are, moreover, strikingly in tune with what was called for by the Vatican Council: a renewal of the Catholic Church that is spiritual, pastoral and ecumenical. The charismatic renewal in the Catholic Church could be looked upon as a response to Vatican II (it did grow out of postconciliar concern for the renewal of the Church), but it could also be said that both the charismatic renewal and the Vatican Council are expressions of the work of the same Spirit endeavoring to renew the church. He is shaping us into a church that will be effective in the second half of the twentieth century.

As we consider what the Lord is doing, we have to keep our vision high enough. Many times the Lord cannot work through us in the way he wants, because we do not expect enough. We see that the Lord is doing something and from that we begin to grasp a vision, but we limit ourselves to a vision that is "realistic," (i.e. one that accepts limitations and obstacles as insurmountable). The Lord wants us to have a vision that answers to faith, not one that is tied down by the obstacles. He wants us to be the kind of people who see what his purpose is and to have faith for all of it, not just what we think is reasonable to hope for. Already the charismatic renewal we are part of has gone far beyond what could reasonably be expected five years ago when it first began.

I believe that we would be seriously mistaken to settle for the idea of a Catholic charismatic movement. The Lord is after something much larger.

He is working among us for the renewal of the whole church. He wishes to bring all Christians to live their lives as Christians in a new way (in new patterns of life) in spiritual power (so that they can change the world) and as one as Jesus and the Father are one (Jn. 17:11, 22). Moreover, he wants this to happen not just among individual Christians, but he wants to renew the church as a body, corporately; that renewal should involve a renewal of each grouping within the church as well. The Lord's power is enough for all the problems and defects of his church (Eph. 5:27).

The Lord does not want just a Catholic Pentecostal Movement. He wants the whole Catholic Church charismatically renewed. He wants every person in the Catholic Church to be baptized in the Spirit and to be experiencing spiritual gifts. Even more, he wants every unit of the church's life to be lived in the Spirit. He wants everything that is done in the church to be formed and guided by the Holy Spirit. The Lord wants to form one body in which Catholics, Orthodox and Protestants find not only the original unity they had but an even greater unity in the Holy Spirit. The Lord, in other words, does not just want individuals "touched by his power" or "blessed". He wants the whole of their lives and the whole life of the church changed. We should expect to see the day when all our popes and bishops are not only good Christian men but men who perform miracles (as we pray for them to do when they are consecrated) and lead the church in charismatic boldness and power. We should look for the time when Christians live together in such unity and

13

power that their problem is not worrying over a lack of response, but instead figuring out how to handle the great numbers, who are drawn to them and who want to serve the Lord. We should expect a church which is everything the Lord wants it to be.

**2. We should move from being identified as "Pentecostals" to being identified as Christians who are discovering how to live and serve "in the Spirit".**

At the moment, those who have been touched by the charismatic renewal are usually known as "the Pentecostals". There are "Catholic Pentecostals" all over the country, meeting in "Pentecostal prayer meetings" and famous for a concern with spiritual gifts and spiritual experiences.

There is a limitation in being known as Pentecostals or in thinking of ourselves as Pentecostals. The term means to other people that this is a group of special Christians. They are like other Christians, but they also have this special "Pentecostal thing". They hold meetings for furthering the Pentecostal thing. At these meetings a person can have special spiritual experiences and learn how to speak in tongues and prophesy. According to this common picture, ordinary Christian life is lived in the parish with other ordinary Christians, but you can meet these Pentecostals if you want and have an optional "extra", some special spiritual experiences which some people might want to have and some others might not.

The picture people have of "the Pentecostals" in some way corresponds to the facts. When the

14

"Catholic Pentecostal Movement" began, it began because of a special concern with the baptism in the Spirit and with spiritual gifts (especially tongues, prophecy and healing). At the moment, the movement is still largely a specialized movement. Although many groups are developing concerns beyond baptism in the Spirit and spiritual gifts, many other groups, possibly the majority, still place their major focus on this specialized area. People who come, come for spiritual experiences. They come to the Pentecostal prayer meeting to find out about the Holy Spirit just as they would come to the Christian Family Movement to find out about family life and apostolate, or to the Catholic Peace Fellowship to find out about Christian pacifism and non-violence. In other words, the Pentecostal meeting is one among a number of specialized groups within the church.

I am not trying to suggest that there is anything wrong with the word "Pentecostal"; it is a good name, and it refers to an essential dimension of Christianity. Nor an I trying to suggest that there is anything wrong with Pentecostal prayer meetings. They have done a great deal to revive the Christian faith in people who had lost it (or lost their enthusiasm for it). Nor do I want to say that people should not make baptism in the Spirit and spiritual gifts a major focus for a while. Some groups make a mistake by moving on too fast and losing what they began with. I am not even trying to say that I think we should not be a specialized movement at this time (as will become clear further on).

What I do want is that we should speak of what is

happening among us in a different way than by identifying ourselves as "Pentecostals" or by speaking of a "Pentecostal movement". "Pentecostal" implies that we want to be a specialized group of people doing a special thing. It does not have to mean that, but as a matter of fact, it does mean that to most people. I do not even think we should refer to ourselves as "charismatics". We ought to refer to ourselves and think of ourselves simply as Christians who have discovered something that is a normal part of Christian life.

When I speak of being baptized in the Spirit and experiencing spiritual gifts as something that is normal for Christians, I do not mean that such things are in fact happening to most Christians. I simply mean that these things are intended to be normal for all Christians: they are according to the norm of what the Christian life should be. All Christians should be baptized in the Spirit and experience spiritual gifts in order to live Christianity in the way Christ intended it to be lived. We are not trying to do something special. We are simply trying to live Christianity in the power of the Spirit.

Does this mean that all Christians have to be Pentecostals in order to be "normal" Christians or full Christians? Yes and no. If by "being Pentecostals" we mean that a person must belong to the specialized movement which has come to be known as "the Pentecostal movement", the answer is no. We have to be very careful not to equate what is happening with us as a group of people (our movement) with the Lord's renewal of his church. The Lord is very free to move outside of the groups of those who acknowledge the name Pentecostal. Moreover, if the movement we are part of is not faithful to following the Lord, he could discard it and continue to renew his church in power without it. The Holy Spirit is indispensable, we are not.

If, on the other hand, we mean by "being Pentecostal" that a person has experienced the change in relationship with the Holy Spirit which we have described with the term "baptized in the Spirit" and that they experience the Holy Spirit working through them in spiritual gifts, the answer is definitely yes. A person has to be a Pentecostal in this sense in order to be a "normal" Christian, a Christian who is living his Christian life according to the norm of the way Christ intended it to be. Our own particular Pentecostal group may not be for every Christian, nor may a lot of the things we do but the new life we are experiencing through this outpouring of his Spirit that we call the charismatic renewal is for everyone.

When we in our community sought the Lord for a name, the name he gave us was "The Word of God" not "The Pentecostal community in Ann Arbor" or something of the sort. We would never have picked that name, but we have since discovered much wisdom in being named that way. One of the reasons it is such a good name is that it allows us to be identified in people's minds as simply a community of Christians. Everyone knows that we are "charismatic" or "Pentecostal". We are proud of the fact, and make no attempt to hide it. But they also know that we are not trying to be "Pentecostals", but Christians, followers of the Lord Jesus Christ.

**3. We should understand what is happening**

**among us as a renewal rather than as a movement.**

At this time, much of the charismatic renewal has the character of a specialized movement. Those involved are people who have discovered in a new way what the Holy Spirit can do. They have found that through expectant faith they can come into a new experiential knowledge of the presence of the Holy Spirit (baptism in the Spirit) and into a new experience of the Holy Spirit working through them to build up the body of Christ (spiritual gifts). They have gathered together with others who have made the same discovery (or who are interested in it), and are forming a rapidly growing movement.

At this stage of its development, the charismatic renewal needs to be a movement (we will discuss this further in a later guideline). This is a new thing that the Lord is doing, and in order for it to grow and develop, people have to begin with a specialized movement. But something more significant is going on than the formation of a movement. God is at work to renew his church completely, in every aspect. And he is pouring out his Spirit to make that possible.

We do not want to equate our movement (the charismatic renewal as it is today) with the renewal of the church. Many other things are happening that are part of God's renewal of his church. But what we have discovered is a very fundamental dimension of any church renewal. We are coming to learn how the presence of the Holy Spirit in the church can be brought to consciousness in people in an effective way; we are also learning how yielding to the work of that Spirit can bring results in Christian life. The work of the Holy Spirit is fundamental; that is, it has to be the basis of everything else in Christian life. The rediscovery of the power of the Spirit, then, is a very fundamental part of church renewal. It has to be at the basis of everything else and it will, of necessity, affect everything else.

The Lord has given the movement we are part of an important role in his work of renewal. He is working through us to help restore an important dimension of Christian life. Our goal should not be to use what the Lord has given us to create a powerful movement that will last through the centuries. Our goal should be to see that new power and life touch the church in all of its aspects. Our goal, in other words, should be the charismatic renewal of the whole church.

The charismatic renewal as a movement (which it now is) should be more like the liturgical movement than like the Christian Family Movement. The Christian Family Movement is a specialized movement in the church, trying to do a specific job. The liturgical movement, however, as a renewal of the public worship of the church, was concerned with a dimension of the life of the church so fundamental that it affected everyone and touched every aspect of church life. Just as the liturgical movement no longer exists as a specific group of people in the church, because the whole church has accepted and developed liturgical renewal, so the charismatic movement should some day cease to exist, because the whole church should accept and develop charismatic renewal.

Part of what charismatic renewal means is extending the new life in the Spirit we are discovering to everyone in the church. However, another aspect is extending it to everything in church life. Everything should be touched by it and brought to newness. This is, as a matter of fact, what is now happening. More and more groups in the charismatic renewal are going beyond a concern for being baptized in the Spirit and spiritual gifts to a concern for the various areas of Christian life: worship and liturgy, community, daily life together, service, evangelism. They are discovering what these areas look like when they are charismatically renewed, that is, when the new power and direction of the Holy Spirit is applied to them.

If we are going to be faithful to the way in which the Lord is teaching us to "charismatically renew" different areas of Christian life, we need an approach to baptism in the Spirit and spiritual gifts that integrates them fully into the Christian life. We should not focus on them, but on the Lord and on following the Lord. We are not interested in spiritual experience in itself or in spiritual gifts in themselves. We are interested in the Lord and in anything that helps us to know, love, and serve the Lord with greater power.

"Charismatic renewal" is a good name to describe what the Lord is doing among us. It draws attention to the fact that what the Lord is about is a renewal of the church. The name itself points us toward our goal.

**4. As we move forward in charismatic renewal, we should be fully of the Catholic Church in our**

**participation and activities in the Catholic Church.**

Nowadays it is easy to become disaffected in relationship to the Catholic Church in our participation and activities in the Catholic Church. This disaffection can come to us from both Catholic and Protestant sources. Today there are many people dissatisfied with the lack of spiritual vitality in all the churches, and this dissatisfaction can lead to an anti-institutionalism and a critical spirit. Sometimes people with this kind of disaffection will agree that it is right to stay within the churches, but they approach their involvement in the churches as if they were a "foreign body" or guerilla band within them. Catholics who have this disaffection often stay in the Catholic Church not because they are "of the Catholic Church" but because they simply want to change it or influence it. They do not belong to it in their heart.

If the Lord is calling us to stay within the Catholic Church (and he is), he is calling us to stay within it from our hearts. He is calling us to be loyal members with a genuine love for the church and a loyalty to its leaders. That does not mean that we cannot see things that are wrong with the church or things that we think should change. That does not mean that we cannot disagree with the leaders of the church or desire a different kind of leadership from them. But it does mean that we must serve within the church as committed members, and not operate like a guerilla band within it.

I believe that the Lord not only wants us to be loyal members of the Catholic Church, but that he also wants us to appreciate the contribution the Catholic Church is meant to make to what he is trying to do among Christians today. We should neither, on the one hand look at Catholicism as an obstacle to Christianity nor, on the other hand defensively try to protect traditional Catholicism against attacks or criticism; we should try to discern what elements of present Catholic life are essential to Christianity and to what the Lord is doing. I would like to suggest the following elements as some of the contributions which the Catholic Church can offer to other Christians that are essential for strengthening the work which the Lord is trying to do today (the list is not intended to be complete or definitive):

—a universality or catholicity: the church is meant to be one body throughout the world that is united in visible bonds of love and order. This sense the Catholic Church has preserved in a vital way.

—a universality in time: the Holy Spirit has never left the church or Christians. Christian teaching has been handed on through the centuries, and we must be in genuine communion with Christian teachers and teaching of all ages. We must, of course, look at Christian history with discernment. Not all that was taught is good teaching. But we need the sense of continuity and universality that the Catholic Church has preserved.

—a "first elder" or "first overseer" (the pope): the present organizational structure of the Catholic Church can certainly be changed in radical ways if that were seen to be good. The present way the papacy operates could also change radically. I suspect both things will have to change somewhat for the pope to become the first shepherd of all Christians. But there is a need for a "first bishop", someone who can be a source of unity for the universal church. The Catholic Church has preserved this office.

— the Eucharist as the center of the life of a Christian community: the Eucharist was meant to be the center of the worship life of Christians and a means by which the Lord can feed us and strengthen us in the life of the Spirit. The Catholic Church has preserved a vital eucharistic life.

The Lord is calling us in the Catholic charismatic renewal to be Christians first of all and this must be our center and focus. But he is calling us to be Christians who are Catholic and charismatic (Pentecostal). Each of the elements described above is integral to Christianity and for what the Lord wants to do.

**5. As we move forward in the charismatic renewal of the church, we should be fostering the unity of all Christians, Catholic, Protestant, Orthodox, in the one Spirit, not reinforcing old divisions.**

Many people have remarked on the extraordinary oneness that can exist among Catholics and Protestants when they gather together in the Holy Spirit. There is a common dedication to the Lord and a true brotherhood as followers of Jesus. Our unity is certainly not complete, and it cannot be complete as long as we are committed to different church bodies that are not yet united. But nonetheless, we do experience a definite God-given unity. In fact, we often experience much more unity, even a greater unity in faith with other Christians involved in the charismatic renewal than we do with other Catholics (mainly because of the widespread loss of faith among many who are still participants in the Catholic Church).

For Catholics and Protestants this new unity can be a very fearful thing. Both have a tendency to want to withdraw back to the security of other Catholic Pentecostals or Lutheran Pentecostals or Conservative Evangelical Pentecostals or Fundamentalist Pentecostals. Few things can be harder than for a Classical Pentecostal to discover that the Catholic Pentecostal brother he has met in the Lord still prays to Mary. Or, a Catholic may be troubled by difficult guilt feelings as he wonders what will happen to some of the things that were inculcated deeply into him as a child in Catholic schools.

Yet, the Vatican Council long ago committed the Catholic Church to ecumenism. It recognized Protestant Christians as "joined with us in the Holy Spirit" (CC 15) and as "brothers in the Lord" (DEcum 3). It even recognized the Protestant churches as "Christian communions" and "ecclesial communities". Not only the individuals but also the bodies have a role in God's plan. Moreover, as we read about the dialogues between Catholic and Lutheran, Reformed and Anglican theologians, most of us feel surprised at how many things they agree upon as being commonly accepted.

Sometimes when Catholics are touched by the work of the Holy Spirit, things are reawakened that were part of an earlier time in their religious life when they were in more touch with the Lord. But new life in the Holy Spirit can reawaken not only devotion to God that was once there, but also Catholic conservatism that was once there. That means that we have to discern what from our past is good and what we need to grow out of. If a Catholic conservatism from our past stands in the way of our doing what the Lord has in mind, we have to overcome it.

If we want to follow what the Lord is doing in the church today and in the charismatic renewal today, we in the Catholic charismatic renewal, have to have an ecumenical concern. The unity with other Christians that we experience is something the Lord wants to have continue. He is moving all Christians towards a oneness of brotherly communion and service, and we should be open to following his leading.

Ecumenical concern means two things for us. It means that although we have a special concern for the renewal of the Catholic Church, we cannot let that concern shut off the future unity between the churches nor the present possibilities of unity between us and Christians in the charismatic renewal who belong to other churches. We should not let old walls grow back up again. Ecumenical concern further means that we have to make the unity of Christians an integral part of our goal. We do not want a Catholic church or a Catholic movement with merely an "ecumenical openness" or "ecumenical overtones". We want to pursue genuine unity. The temptation here is to think that such unity cannot come, or if it does come it cannot be achieved in a good way (too many valuable things would have to be sacrificed for it to be worth-while). But if we have faith in the Lord, we must believe that he has the power to bring that unity into existence without losing any of the fullness of Christianity. We should not limit the Lord by our lack of faith in him.

# TODAY:
# A MOVEMENT FOR
# CHARISMATIC
# RENEWAL

We want to keep our vision clear so that we do not block the Lord's work by our narrowness of view or our lack of faith. But we also want to see where we are now and what it is sensible to do in the present situation. A vision is meant to enlighten our path, not blind us so that we cannot take the next step. The long-range vision is of all Christians living the life of the Spirit in power united in one body with all other Christians throughout the world. The present step is a Catholic charismatic renewal that is patterned and directed in such a way that it can move towards the vision the Lord seems to be setting before us.

**6. For a while to come there should be an international movement for charismatic renewal in the Catholic Church.**

Guidelines three and four might seem to indicate that we should simply merge into the Catholic Church without being a distinct movement at all. Guideline five might point in the direction of forming one movement for charismatic renewal in all the churches. But the Lord is blessing the Catholic charismatic renewal right now and giving it an extraordinary power and authority both within the Catholic Church and among other Christians, those involved in the charismatic renewal and those not involved in the charismatic renewal. There are real reasons for the existence of an international movement for charismatic renewal in the Catholic Church at the moment.

In order to see the reasons for movement for charismatic renewal in the Catholic Church, we must consider two separate questions. The first question is: Why have a distinct movement and not simply merge into the Catholic Church? The second question is: Why have a specifically Catholic movement and not have an ecumenical charismatic renewal?

To begin with, there are reasons for having a distinct movement within the Catholic Church right now. A first reason is our own need to grow in the life of the Spirit. If there were no special meetings or activities in the church that were explicitly charismatic or dedicated to the charismatic renewal, we would not be able to move forward in this new dimension with the same rapidity and depth. Being baptized in the Spirit and exercising spiritual gifts are so new to us that we need to come together and learn about them together. We also need to come together and explore the implications of these new experiences for the whole life of the Catholic Church: parish structure, religious education, liturgy, apostolate. We need to come together to discover the full implications of what the Holy Spirit is doing among us and to discover what wineskins are needed for the new wine.

A second reason for a distinct movement within the Catholic Church is the value it has in bringing to Catholics today an appreciation of what it means to be baptized in the Spirit, to live in the Spirit, and to use spiritual gifts. Catholics must have gatherings of people at which they can learn about these things and receive help in finding them for themselves. Moreover, the very existence of such a movement calls attention to the reality and gains a hearing for it.

There is a third reason for having a distinct movement for charismatic renewal within the church. Through such a movement, we give witness to the reality of Christ and the possibility of knowing him by experience. In the crisis of faith in the church today (especially in the United States) there are few

29

groups maintaining a forceful witness to the Lord. The very strength and vitality of our movement says that the Lord is alive. The movement seems to have a definite effect in recalling the many Catholics in the country to a concern for spiritual renewal.

There are also several reasons for having a movement for charismatic renewal in the Catholic Church and not just having an ecumenical movement. One good reason is that Catholics can reach Catholics and a Catholic movement can reach the Catholic Church. Christians have not yet reached the point where most of their Christian lives are lived with Christians of other churches. Most Catholics still have contact only with other Catholics when they come together for Christian purposes. The same is true of most Lutherans, most Presbyterians and so on. It does seem that there will be a time when Christians will be coming together more in ecumenical groupings. This time is already here among young Christians and among Christians concerned for renewal. But at the moment most Christians are grouped by church, and a Catholic charismatic renewal is in the position to serve the existing Catholic groupings and to reach the Catholics in those groupings.

A second reason for having a Catholic movement and not just an ecumenical one is the opportunity to draw on Catholic tradition and Catholic life. As was considered in guideline four, the Catholic Church has an important contribution to make to what the Lord is doing today. The riches of Catholic tradition and the values of Catholic life can achieve a new vitality in Catholic charismatic meetings and

30

groupings. Someday those same riches and values will be able to be appreciated within ecumenical meetings and all Christians will be able to accept them. That day is beginning now (in a miraculous way), but it is not yet here to the degree that we could have an ecumenical movement alone without losing many valuable things.

A third reason is this: a Catholic movement can serve the corporate renewal of the Catholic Church better than an ecumenical one. The Lord wants to renew the church as a body and not just individuals within it. As long as the Catholic Church is not joined to all the other Christian churches, it must be renewed corporately, as a body. Only a Catholic movement can serve in that way.

Being a Catholic and having a Catholic movement does not mean being closed to ecumenical concern. There is a growing and deepening communication between Catholics who are dedicated to the charismatic renewal of the Catholic Church and other Christians who are dedicated to the charismatic renewal of their own churches. There are also many groups with ecumenical membership participating in activities of the Catholic charismatic renewal. The existence of a Catholic charismatic renewal can serve the wider charismatic renewal as a distinct movement if it develops with the kind of openness and concern for others that the Lord wants.

**7. For a while to come, there should be groups and meetings whose primary focus is charismatic renewal.**

It is well to say that our goal should be the

charismatic renewal of the church as a whole, in fact, the complete renewal of Christian life. Yet, as we saw in the previous guidelines, we have need right now for a movement which can be the bearer of charismatic renewal for the whole church. If that is true, we need groups and meetings whose primary focus is charismatic renewal in order to make the movement for charismatic renewal possible.

Normally, charismatic renewal begins when a group of people who have been baptized in the Spirit gather together to seek a deeper life in Christ. They tend to focus on a number of things which are new to them and have come to them through the charismatic renewal: baptism in the Spirit, spiritual gifts, (especially tongues, prophecy and healing), praise and worship of God, growing in faith, being led by the Spirit, sometimes deliverance, sometimes community.

As different "charismatic renewal groups" begin to develop, they usually take one of two forms:
a) prayer groups: most groups become prayer groups which meet once a week and are fairly small. They center on nourishing the spiritual life of their members in a charismatic way.
b) "regional renewal centers": some groups become quite large, often fairly quickly. They become a center for a city or region. Many people come to them and from them will grow many prayer groups and occasionally communities of special works of service.

As these prayer groups and regional renewal centers form, different things begin to happen with each group. Some of them develop into communities or special forms of service. These we will consider in guideline nine. Groups which develop in this way are in the minority, and probably should be in the minority. The Lord has different purposes for different groups. Even though there are advantages to developing into a community or into a special form of service, the conditions are often not right for such a development. The Lord's path may not be ours. We should be patient, seek his guidance, and follow him in whatever way he works.

Of the groups which do not develop into communities or special forms of service, few stay in existence for very long. Prayer groups and regional renewal centers can be unstable. That is however not at all a bad thing. The Lord does not necessarily intend all such groups to have a very long existence. He has a purpose for each group. Some groups, for instance, are only meant by God to exist long enough to introduce some people to a deeper life in the Spirit. Some groups may only be intended to exist long enough to give birth to a group that the Lord does want to develop. Our concern should not be to prolong the existence of our group, but to serve the Lord. If the Lord's purpose for our group is over, we should move on the way he wants us to.

Sometimes prayer groups can and should last for a length of time, but should never develop into a community or into such service. Such prayer groups provide spiritual nourishment and support for the members, but do not and should not do much more. When this is the case, it is important for the members of the group to become integrated into a parish or some other Christian organization in such a way that the resources of the group are supplemented and the members of the group find good outlets for Christian service. If the spiritual life that is being nourished in the prayer group does not find an outlet in service and open out into concern for larger groups of Christians, it will stagnate.

At the moment prayer groups and regional renewal centers are the main form that charismatic renewal is taking. Most people who are involved in charismatic renewal are involved in such groups. Prayer groups and regional renewal centers have an important role to play in the Lord's work right now. They should be respected and fostered.

**8. The international movement for charismatic renewal should evolve from being a specialized movement to a movement for the restoration of full Christian life.**

A specialized movement for charismatic renewal has a purpose in this stage of the Lord's plan. The newer the movement, and the closer it lies to its beginnings, the more it must center on the "charismatic basics" (baptism in the Spirit, spiritual gifts). But movements are alive and growing. They do not stay in one place. And what is true of secular movements is even more true of movements that are inspired by God's Spirit. If the movement for charismatic renewal is to remain healthy, it has to move on in the right way.

All movements have stages. They begin with a spreading enthusiasm for an ideal. Something new comes, and people are attracted to it. They begin to accept the new ideal and begin to gather together with others who are also attracted to it. The liturgical movement began as a spreading interest and enthusiasm for a renewal in the public worship of the church. The civil rights movement began as a spreading concern and enthusiasm for equal rights for all Americans. Every movement in history, spiritual or secular, has such a beginning stage.

At first the enthusiasm for the ideal alone seems to sustain the new movement, creating a remarkable unity among the people involved in it. But soon other factors begin to make themselves felt. It becomes clear that in order for the ideal to make headway in the world, it must be translated into the terms of a concrete, visible reality; it must actually be lived out from day to day. Different groups within the movement begin to develop their own special approaches for relating the ideal to the rest of life. In the liturgical movement, a variety of different approaches to Church renewal developed: not only liturgical conferences, but also catechetical programs and scriptural institutes. In the civil rights movement, different groups like the NAACP, SNCC, CORE, and the Black Power movement arose.

This is the second stage of a movement, and it seems to be an inevitable change. The development can lead to splits and fragmentations in the movement (as happened to some degree in the civil rights movement) or to a unified movement with a fuller approach or a variety of complementary approaches (as happened in the liturgical movement). The change itself, however, seems inevitable, because the implications of the ideal must be explored and worked out.

The Catholic charismatic renewal is already in the

second stage. Different approaches are appearing. Prayer groups and renewal centers are the predominant form the renewal is taking, but various sorts of communities and works of service with varying approaches are already beginning to appear. It is therefore important for us to look to the future and see how the Lord wants the movement for charismatic renewal to develop as it grows out of the first stage.

The Catholic charismatic renewal cannot remain a movement which is concerned only with baptism in the Spirit and spiritual gifts. The intrinsic dynamic of the situation is moving us on. The new life in the Spirit we are discovering demands that every aspect of Christian life be changed. We seem to be increasingly led to a concern for a renewal of all of Christian life and a restoration of everything that is missing. The different approaches that are developing are examples of ways in which charismatic renewal is being applied to different areas of church life.

Although we cannot avoid being moved on, we do have an option in how we respond. We can either split into a variety of different movements and groups, or we can keep a unified movement that is open to growing into a movement for the restoration of full Christian life. The history of the civil rights movement or the Classical Pentecostal movement show how easily we could split into different groups, that could even become hostile to one another. Neither unity nor disunity is inevitable. We must choose one and work towards it.

I believe that the Lord wants us to work towards

one broad movement for the restoration of full Christian life rather than to let ourselves become a variety of movements with different approaches - mainly because of the need of the church. The church is in great need today of a movement that is flexible, but that is solidly spiritual and united in its dedication to Christ and in its concern for Christian renewal. Were we unable to stay united, we would be less able to be the sort of instrument the Lord needs for the Christian renewal of the church.

A choice is being made in the Catholic Church (and in the other Christian churches). Among both those who are holding on to a more traditional faith in Christ and those who are advocating a secular or secular humanist version of Christianity, there is a lack of enthusiasm and hope. As attendance drops off, good candidates for the priesthood become scarcer, and the young disappear, the whole church is losing life.

As we look at the situation within the church and the need of the church, our unity becomes of much more importance. We must maintain as much unity as possible among all the groups and individuals who are committed to faith in Christ as the basis of the life of the church, but we should also work to keep as much unity as possible in our own movement for charismatic renewal. Perhaps our greatest service will prove to be our existence as a strong Christian movement of people who have a living faith in Christ and an enthusiasm and hope in serving him. The more united we are, the stronger a force we can be in the Christian renewal of the church and in a restoration of morale among those who are members of the church.

There is room for many approaches, and different situations will need different approaches. But, the Lord does want a unity among all those who are dedicated to serving him and to following him. There should be a oneness of spirit among us, a bond of peace. That unity will give us greater power to strengthen the church in the Lord and to bring the world to him.

**9. We should move from forming groups whose primary focus is charismatic renewal towards shouldering the day-in, day-out work of nurturing Christian life.**

The prayer groups and "regional renewal centers" that are the main type of grouping in the charismatic renewal now are specialized groups. Their primary focus is on "charismatic life", especially on baptism in the Spirit and spiritual gifts. Beyond a weekly meeting, sometimes two, and some basic instructional sessions, all centering on spirituality and on the things which are special emphases in the charismatic renewal, there is little to their life together.

Because charismatic groups are specialized, the people who come to them are dependent on many other "non-charismatic" things to foster their Christian lives. They come to the prayer meeting to refurbish the spiritual side of their Christian life. Then, for most of the things they need as Christians, they take part in parish activities. If they want their children educated as Christians, they send them to the usual parish CCD programs which do not normally introduce the children to a deeper life in the

Spirit. If they want to work apostolically, they join apostolic organizations which usually proceed without looking for the guidance or the power of the Spirit in the way charismatic groups are learning to do. Most of their Christian lives, in other words, will be lived in situations untouched by the charismatic renewal. That is because charismatic groups usually are not yet able to provide more of the day-in day-out work that goes into nurturing Christian life and fostering Christian service.

For many of us, specialized charismatic renewal groups are the right places for us to be. Any further Christian help we need or outlets for Christian service that we are ready for should come through the normal means of church life (probably parish activities). But if the charismatic renewal is going to develop properly and make the kind of contribution it can and should make to the life of the church, more and more charismatic groups will need to shoulder more of the day-in day-out work of the church. As the charismatic renewal evolves, many of the different groups formed to promote charismatic renewal should evolve to the point where they can make a greater contribution to church life than just helping people be baptized in the Spirit, yield to spiritual gifts, and grow to some degree in spirituality. There seem to be two main ways (each of which can be expressed in a variety of approaches) in which the Lord is leading some people within the charismatic renewal to make use of what they have found for the work of the church: forming communities and developing works of service.

At the moment the Lord seems to be calling a

number of groups to form communities. In a community, people live for and serve the Lord together, as a body, with their lives in common. Communities are able to undertake much of the work of helping people live their daily lives as Christians, and communities are not just restricted to helping the "spiritual lives" of their members as most prayer groups are. Communities can provide instruction in Christian living, programs for children and young people, means of family renewal, evangelism, help to people with special problems, and any forms of service which people need to live a full Christian life. As communities form and develop, more and more aspects of Christian life are touched by the power of the Spirit and more and more needs that Christians have can be supplied. Christians are not forced to come to a special Pentecostal meeting for their spirituality and then look to programs and institutions that have not been renewed spiritually for other needs. They can find their charismatic life integrated into a full concern for all of Christian life.

There are a variety of ways that such communities can be related to the rest of the church. They can form:

a) in one Catholic parish as a special community within that parish;

b) in one Catholic parish as the heart of the renewal of that parish and as something used by the pastors of that parish for the whole parish;

c) with people from a number of Catholic parishes, providing renewal for all the parishes in an area;

d) with people from Catholic parishes and Protestant churches, providing renewal for all the churches in an area;

e) as a non-territorial parish providing an alternative way of life to the normal parish.

If our goal is to renew the whole church, such communities, however they are formed, should always be in a good relationship to the existing church structures and should always seek to be a source of service and new life to them. They should not just go their own way.

But community life is not the only way to integrate the charismatic renewal into the full life of the church. At the moment there are also a number of groups of people involved in the charismatic renewal who have undertaken to provide various services: to provide centers for retreats and renewal weekends, to establish spiritual counseling centers, to form evangelistic teams, to establish programs for young people, to establish special centers to help people on drugs or in alcoholism or other special problems. People have seen a need and have come together to meet that need, making use of the new power they have found in the life of the Spirit.

There are a variety of ways in which such works of service can form and be effective:
a) by working out of a larger charismatic community as a special service of that community (or occasionally, working out of a prayer group);
b) by forming a group especially to perform such a service, without being part of a larger community;
c) by a group that is already performing a service becoming involved in the charismatic renewal;
d) by people who are part of a religious order or

congregation forming special charismatic houses within that order or congregation which take on a special service or form a center for spiritual renewal.

There are many ways in which charismatic groups can undertake services which will further the work of the church. These, like communities that form, should always be in a good relationship to existing church structures and similar efforts by other Christians. They should always avoid charismatic one-upsmanship.

Most of the approaches that have been described above presuppose that the community or work of service is something which evolves out of charismatic groups that were originally drawn by an interest in the charismatic renewal. A few, however, involve groups that are already in existence— parishes, religious communities or other Christian groups - that enter the charismatic renewal as a group and go forward in a new way. I suspect we will see more groups which already exist becoming charismatic as the charismatic renewal becomes more and more accepted. But there are fewer of them right now for a good reason: it is more difficult to take a previously existing group and make such a change than to form a whole new group out of people who are willing to make a commitment to the charismatic renewal. Already existing groups, in order to make a successful change, must reach the point where two things have happened: 1) all the members of the group are willing to commit themselves individually and as a group to charismatic renewal; 2) all the members of the group are willing to make changes in the patterns of life of the group to make the group life more "charismatic". Until these things happen explicitly, the group cannot move forward as a charismatic group. These things can rarely happen without having some of the older members of the group leave (perhaps by transfer to a different parish, convent or chapter of whatever group it may be).

The outpouring of the Spirit which we are experiencing is for a deepening of our daily life as Christians and for a strengthening of our power to serve. It is for a renewal of the Church. The Lord wants us to grow to the point where we can make greater use of the new life and power he has given us to shoulder the daily work of building Christian life. As we do, not only will the life of the Christian people become stronger but more Christians will begin to see that our concern is not just special spiritual phenomena but the normal equipment of the Christian people to live as Christians effectively.

**10. The charismatic renewal should exist as a movement primarily through gatherings for growth in the life of the Spirit and through services which encourage the life of the Spirit.**

A movement is primarily people who want something or are advocating something. The present movement for charismatic renewal consists of those who believe that the Lord is willing to give his Spirit in an experiential way and restore the spiritual gifts that were part of the New Testament church and who want these things for themselves. But a movement can also be seen in terms of the things which allow those people to come together or to be united and in communication with one another. Now, the movement for charismatic renewal exists through gatherings which draw people together and the services which foster the new life in the Spirit.

Gatherings which support and foster the charismatic renewal are regional and national. The regional gatherings have been Days of Renewal, Leaders' Days (Service Days), regional conferences and "Charismatic" or "Pentecostal" retreats or weekends. On the national level, there has been "the June Conference" (the International Conference for Charismatic Renewal) and the leaders conferences (the National Service Conference, the regional service conferences). These gatherings have been dedicated to learning how to be baptized in the Spirit, how to live in the Spirit, how to grow in spiritual gifts. They have, in other words, been "Pentecostal" gatherings primarily concerned with the work of the Spirit. But they have also been gradually widening their concern to more and more aspects of Christian life.

Services which have supported and fostered the charismatic renewal are books, newsletters, magazines, and speakers. Many of these function on the regional level: New Covenant, Dove Publications, Charismatic Renewal Books, Charismatic Renewal Cassettes, and a growing pool of speakers. These services, like the gatherings, have been primarily centered on the charismatic dimension, but are opening out to a wider concern for the full Christian life.

The American tendency is immediately to

structure a movement by establishing a national organization, with presidents, officials, fees (dues), business meetings, regulations and memberships. There often comes a time when a more formal national organization is of value in being able to respond to what the Lord is doing. And there are other, more spiritual, ways of structuring a national organization than the usual American way. The liabilities we see in most national organizations do not have to be part of a national organization for the charismatic renewal. At this point in the charismatic renewal, however, we probably are not ready for a national (much less international) organization. At the moment an informal movement of the kind we have, fed by gatherings and services, seems to be the best form for the charismatic renewal in the Catholic Church. It allows for a maximum flexibility as we try to discern how the Lord is working in and through the charismatic renewal. It may always be the best form. At this point, it seems too soon to tell whether anything more might be needed in the future.

**11. The working structure of the charismatic renewal should be based on services performed, not on a formal organization.**

Every movement needs some kind of working structure if it is to survive. However, having a "working structure" and having a "formal organization" are not necessarily the same thing. Formal organizations would be essential if there were to be some kind of a national organization as considered in guideline 10. The formal organization of a group of people is based upon the ceding of certain decision making rights to a central agency. That agency then has the authority to make binding decisions. Sometimes the agency can make decisions which determine the life of every member or every grouping in the movement, as in the official structure of the Catholic Church. Sometimes the agency can only make decisions for what happens on the national level. For instance, the National Secretariat of the Cursillo Movement is a national organization. The National Secretariat cannot make decisions about how a local center is to be run: it cannot determine when Cursillos are to be put on or who is going to be in charge. But it can make decisions about the national movement: it decides what the national conferences will be like, what kind of literature is to be published, when national workshops are to be put on.

The kind of working structure which has been evolving in the charismatic renewal is not a formal organization, but rather a kind of service structure. The typical pattern has been as follows: a group of people or a community feels that God is calling them to provide that service and let people know that it is available. If it is a good service, people make use of it and support it. If it is not, it does not survive. It is the services which provide a structure for the national movement.

Service structures have authority, even though they cannot make binding decisions. Their authority comes mainly from the authority in a service well performed (which is sometimes greater than the authority to make binding decisions). Sometimes their authority comes from the need for unity (it is better to work with one Day of Renewal or one international conference and try to improve it than to compete with it and destroy the unity of the movement in an area).

Within the Catholic Charismatic Renewal, the Catholic Charismatic Renewal Service Committee has performed a special role in caring for the unity and strength of the whole movement. The existence of the Service Committee and the way the Committee works has helped the Catholic Charismatic Renewal grow and relate to the Catholic Church in a specially effective way. But the Catholic Charismatic Renewal Service Committee does not operate as a formal organization. It operates only as a committee that provides important services for the movement. This is clearly expressed in its statement of purpose:

"The Catholic Charismatic Renewal Service Committee (CCRSC) does not exist to plan a renewal, but it exists to be of service to a renewal that God is bringing about. It is attempting to discern what the Lord is doing, and to make specific contributions to the Lord's work, the contributions which the committee sees that the Lord is equipping it for and leading it to make.

"The purpose of the CCRSC is not to organize a movement, to oversee a movement, or to make money. Its purpose is to provide services for the charismatic renewal of the Church . . .

"The CCRSC is a committee which does not claim any authority over groups or individuals involved in the charismatic renewal of the Church. Its only authority is over the services it provides, and within those services it exercises the normal supervision . . .

"Because the charismatic renewal is a renewal (an unorganized movement), there can be no authority structure within it. The only authority can be the authority that comes from services well performed. The acceptance of the services provided by CCRSC is the test of its success."

There may be a time when it would be good to have some kind of national organization for the charismatic renewal. But it does seem that a service structure is fitted to the present life of the movement. The key to its success is a concern for unity and a commitment to one another in love. In an atmosphere of love and unity, different services can strengthen the one movement of the Spirit. Without that atmosphere, much of the present strength of the national movement would drain away or be used for competition or strife. The task of those who provide any services in the movement is to preserve unity within the movement and peace with those in the churches who are not in the movement.

# PRESERVING LOVE AND UNITY

The Catholic Charismatic Renewal is a movement in which two streams of Christian life intersect: the Catholic Church and the modern charismatic movement. Those of us who are involved in the Catholic charismatic renewal find ourselves members of two Christian bodies: the largest Christian church in the world and a very dynamic movement involving people from all the churches. We can provide a link or a bridge between these two groups which would otherwise be in little contact with one another. The Lord has placed us in a situation where we can provide a powerful service of unity among the Christian people.

In order for us to provide the kind of service which the Lord seems to be calling us to, we have to take an active concern for three relationships. We have to be concerned for the love and unity within the Catholic charismatic renewal itself. We have to be concerned for our relationship with other members of the Catholic Church. And we have to be concerned for our relationship with other Christians involved in the charismatic movement who are not Catholics. We have a serious responsibility to keep each link of the chain strong.

**12. To avoid divisiveness within the movement due to pluralism of approaches, we should:**

   **a) have a loose structure which gives no one binding authority over anyone else in the international movement.**

   **b) discourage all tendencies to deal with issues of approach in an ideological way.**

As the charismatic renewal develops, there is a tendency for a variety of approaches to develop (see guideline 8). As we move into a more mature stage of the movement, we need to deal with the problem of pluralism in approaches to the life of the Spirit. For instance, there are disagreements as to whether tongues is for everyone or not, disagreements about whether God wants everyone to be healed or some people to suffer, disagreements about whether it is better to be "free in the Spirit" (i.e. have much expressiveness) or to be "more contemplative" (i.e. be quieter and more restrained). Such disagreements could wreck any kind of national unity. Historically, they have kept groups of non-Catholic Pentecostals separated from each other, sometimes in hostility. When we see the magnitude of what we agree on and how much the Church needs it, we can see that we have to allow enough room for diversity in other things, even those that are important.

**a) We should have a loose structure which gives no one binding authority over anyone else in the international movement.**

The first guidelines for avoiding divisiveness due to pluralism in approaches - the loose structure - has been described in the previous two guidelines. Such a structure allows each group to pursue its own distinctive approach. If a group feels that its way is more in accordance with God's plan than their brothers' way (or if they feel it is at least more suited for their own situation) they try it out and see if the Lord works through them more. In such a structure there is a minimal opening for politics or power struggle.

A more formal organization does not necessarily mean that there cannot be a pluralism of approaches. Those who are responsible for a formal organization can allow, even foster, a pluralism of approaches. But in order for that to happen, there must be a worked-out understanding of how to approach the pluralism and of how much uniformity there will be. With the kind of movement we have at

51

the moment, it is probably better not to have to come to such an understanding, but simply to have a structure that is informal and involves no binding authority.

**b) We should discourage all tendencies to deal with issues of approach in an ideological manner.**

Equally important for avoiding a divisiveness due to pluralism in approaches is to keep all discussion in the area of approaches free from an ideological manner. "Ideology" can mean two different things. "An ideology" can simply be the theory or the general statement behind a movement. There can be a charismatic ideology, a Catholic ideology (Catholic doctrine), a Fundamentalist ideology. "Ideology", defined in this way, is good, in fact essential. A good ideology can be a real help to the Lord's work.

We often, however, use the word "ideological" or the phrase "in an ideological manner" in a somewhat different way. We often mean by ideology those things which a person is not open to discussing, those things which are absolute principles for him. All of us, if we are Christians, take some things in an ideological way. That Jesus is Lord is an absolute principle for us. We are not open to discussing it, at least not willing to discuss it as if we were open to reconsidering it.

There is, however, a tendency to take approaches to working or principles of working as ends in themselves, as absolute values, rather than as means or as insights of limited application. When something is taken in an ideological manner, it becomes an issue which cannot be discussed together - it can only be debated or fought about. In the area of the gift of tongues, for instance, some might maintain that the position of "tongues for all" or "tongues as the initial evidence" is identical with the life of the Spirit. They then feel that to surrender that view is a denial of the Lord himself, or at least a matter of very serious disobedience. Such an attitude makes their view into a matter of ideology, that is, an absolute principle. Others might maintain that it is possible to take different approaches in the area without disobeying the Lord. What is really at issue here is which approach more accurately reflects the actual operation of the gift of tongues in the life of the Spirit. That can be judged by experience (keeping as faithful as possible to what we can see about the area in the Scriptures). By approaching the question (of tongues) in this way, we can avoid considering it in an ideological manner.

In order to work on and live with differences in the area of approach, we should avoid an ideological manner and instead adopt an experimental attitude, open to the results of research and practice, open to being taught by the Spirit and by other men. We should make an effort to have our approaches to a task validated by experience (what bears fruit, what the Lord is working through today) rather than by some personal ideal of heavenly order. (This does not mean, of course, that we rule out the existence of a pattern for working in the scripture or in tradition that we should be faithful to.) Going along with an experimental attitude to matters of approach, we should in any regional, national, and international gatherings try to leave feedom for different approaches to coexist and develop. We should discourage any tendency to excommunicate each other over these issues or to divide because of them.

In short, we should avoid all strife and party spirit (which are works of the flesh - Gal. 5:20) and seek instead the fruit of the Spirit. "Let not him who eats despise him who abstains, and let not him who abstains pass judgement on him who eats; for God has welcomed him. Who are you to pass judgement on the servant of another? . . . Let us then pursue what makes for peace and for mutual upbuilding" (Rom. 14:3-4, 19). In a Church which is being torn by ideological disputes, we should avoid adding new ones of our own. If a large movement can preserve the fruit of the Spirit in its internal life, that would be a genuine testimony to the presence of the Spirit among us.

**13. To avoid divisiveness within the movement due to conflict in the church today, we should:**
   **a) focus on the contribution we make to the church by fostering the life of the Spirit**
   **b) avoid dealing with issues of ecclesiastical policy within the movement.**

Because we are a specialized movement, we have a certain freedom. We can choose what we will be concerned with and what we will take responsibility for. A bishop has to take responsibility for everything that concerns the life of his people. A diocesan newspaper has to be concerned with everything that affects the life of the diocese. The very position they are in forces them to concern themselves with matters simply because these things affect the people that the bishop or the diocesan newspaper serve (to use only two examples). A movement is free to limit its area of concern precisely because it is not responsible for the whole life of a people. It is only attempting to serve people in a specialized way.

As long as we are following the Lord and as long as the Lord wants us to be a specialized movement for charismatic renewal, we are acting properly when we choose to limit our responsibilities to certain areas. As the Lord moves us on to take a wider concern for the restoration of Christian life, we will be less and less free to narrow our concern. At the moment, however, we still have quite a bit of freedom, and we should not be over-eager to take on more than the Lord has yet entrusted to us.

### a) We should focus on the contribution we make to the church by fostering the life of the Spirit.

There seem to be two main areas of conflict in the Catholic Church today. The most significant one is faith. More and more people are losing faith in the reality of Christ or in his importance in the modern world. This area should not cause any problems of disunity in our movement. Probably the main reason why the Lord is pouring out his Spirit so freely today is to meet the problems of loss of faith, and if we cannot be united here, we have no reason to exist.

The second main area of conflict in the church today is in the area of church authority and structure. This is the area which divides people into Liberals and Conservatives and which leads them to engage in various forms of ecclesiastical politics (including extreme measures like authoritarian repression and confrontation tactics). The charismatic renewal will have something to say in this area I believe; but it is not likely that we can expect a consensus in this area for a long time. It is the lack of such a consensus that we will have to deal with.

We have to make first things first. Christ has to come first and knowing how to live with him must be the center of our concern. The more we focus on the Lord and on learning how to live the life of the Spirit, the stronger our unity will be. The life of the Spirit is fundamental enough to provide a base of unity broad enough to bring together radicals and reactionaries in a real unity of spirit. Besides, the need in the church for spiritual renewal is a task great enough to absorb most of our energies for a while. In this context our divisions should not be nearly as painful or bitter. On this foundation, we can begin to learn how the Lord wants these issues approached.

**b) We should avoid dealing with issues of ecclesiastical policy within the movement.**

We should make it a policy in the movement to avoid focusing on hotly disputed or controversial questions. We should make it a policy to avoid having anyone advocating special causes, though still allowing a wide range of expressions and encouraging tolerance. In other words, at meetings of the charismatic renewal, people should not give speeches ("sharings") advocating rights for priests in the church, nor say prayers that God might change Bishop X's mind (or heart), but they should feel free to pray for a particular priest or group of priests who are disputing with their bishops. Or, people should not give exhortations on how we must preach Garabandal, nor pray that the pastor will relent and put the statue of the Immaculate Heart back in the church, they could, however, feel free to lead a prayer of reparation to the Sacred Heart. In other words, people should be allowed to express their lives as Christians, and we should be able to accept that, but they should not use the movement as a forum for their special opinions.

Because we are a specialized group, we can and should avoid most issues that individuals and communities often have to take a stand on. As the Lord leads us to grow into a fuller vision of Christian renewal, we will have to deal with more issues and more problems. That is part of growing up. But now we do not have to allow others to pressure us into taking a stand as a group on controversial or problem areas. All we have to speak about is what we are together for and united on - matters pertaining directly to the life of the Spirit.

**14. To avoid divisions from other Catholics or from the Church as a whole, we should:**

    **a) avoid anything that may call into question our loyalty as Catholics**

    **b) support with discernment current Church structures**

    **c) keep those in the Church who are over us informed of what is happening with us**

    **d) stay free of non-Catholic cultural baggage, and at the same time not neglect to receive**

**new things which are improvements in our old culture.**

If we are going to maintain a commitment to the Catholic Church and the renewal of the Catholic Church, we have to be part of the life of the Catholic Church in an authentic way. We cannot become a "foreign body" in the Church or we will lose our chance to serve the Lord's work of renewal in the Church. Being part of the life of the Catholic Church means more than just the minimum (weekly attendance at Sunday mass, parish membership, regular frequenting of the sacraments). It means also being within the Church and within its life the way other people who are loyal, committed Catholics are. We will be most effective, in fact, when we are active participants in Catholic life and culture.

**a) We should avoid anything that may call into question our loyalty as Catholics**

Guideline 4 said, "As we move forward in the charismatic renewal, we should be fully of the Catholic Church in our participation and activities in the Catholic Church". Just as we need a commitment of our heart to being one with others in the Catholic charismatic renewal, we need a commitment of our heart to being one with other Catholics and with the Catholic Church as a whole. Loyalty or faithfulness is a fruit of the Spirit, and we should be genuinely loyal in our relation with the Church.

Our loyalty has to be expressed in our life together. As a movement within the Roman Catholic Church, we must make it a serious concern to be loyal to the Roman Catholic Church and to the Roman Catholic bishops. This does not mean that as a movement we have to back up everything the bishops do. But it does mean that as a movement we must support the life of the church and its leaders. As a movement we cannot allow anything that is unorthodox in doctrine or that is in opposition to the present policy of the church. There is, of course, a need for wisdom and good judgement to know what is loyal, healthy disagreement of the sort that is a genuine service to the church and its leaders, and what is, on the other hand, opposition to its present policies. But nonetheless, as long as we desire to serve as a movement within the church, we should refrain from anything that is an expression of opposition to its leaders.

To say that we should do these things **as a movement** does not mean that we should insist that all those who take part in the movement should adopt the same policy. As individuals they are free to believe what they want or to take whatever stands they want (they are free to do so from the movement's point of view, that is) as long as they do not speak in the name of the movement. A movement is not called upon to answer for the lives of its members except insofar as they are participating in activities of the movement.

In order to avoid anything that might call into question our loyalty as Catholics in our life as a movement we must avoid anything in our meetings or services as a group which is unorthodox or which might seem disloyal to the church or the bishops. Many different people can come to our meetings or write and speak through our services. But they must understand that they are participating in something that is Catholic. Their actions must not be allowed to compromise our place as a movement in the Catholic Church.

### b) We should support with discernment current church structures

We must do something more than just avoid anything that might call into question our loyalty as Catholics. Loyalty means that we have to go beyond that and actively support the life of the church. Moreover, we have to actively support the life of the church insofar as it is a body, a corporate entity, and not just insofar as it is a number of individuals. Our support of the church has to be a support of its common life, which means its presently existent structures, especially the parish and the diocese.

There are two extremes that we could get into in relating to the present structures and life of the church. One is to avoid them completely, seeking to live our Christian lives completely in special groups that have little relationship to the present structures and only making contact with the official structures of the church when necessary (to fulfil our Sunday Mass obligation, to have our children baptized, etc.). The other is the "plunge in and renew" approach: getting as involved as possible with our parish or with some Catholic organization, expecting that now that we have been baptized in the Spirit, we will be bringing new life. Neither approach works very well. The first means that we end up not serving the church because we have no real involvement with it. The second means that we do not help the church very much because we become involved in situations which take up much of our time and where we do not have much freedom to work for new life.

A better option is to support present structures, but with discernment. There is no obligation to get involved with the men's club just because it is there or needs help, nor is there any obligation to teach in a CCD program where we have no freedom to teach about Christianity but must go along with a program designed to inculcate secular humanism. But there are few situations in the church where we cannot make some genuine contribution. More often than not, there is some place in the CCD program where we can effectively serve, either where the program is a good, genuinely Christian program or where we have the freedom to find a good, genuinely Christian way to teach. Or there is some other program or activity in the parish in which we can take part in and feeling that we are making a genuinely Christian contribution.

Most of the time there is nothing wrong with choosing where we will serve. It is important to do so, in fact. Much of the present activity in the Church does not contribute to the renewal of the Church. If we work in it, we are keeping something alive that should pass away, and we are taking up time that we could use productively. There are many needs in the Church today. We should try and discern what contribution the Lord wants us to make, and make it.

We should not fall into the attitude that our work in groups connected with the charismatic renewal is not a way of serving the life of the Church or the present structures of the Church. It is true, there are some situations in which our charismatic prayer group is clearly viewed as being outside of the parish or of the diocese; therefore, in order to support the life of the church, we are expected to do other things. But in principle this should not be the case. In our charismatic groups, we are concerned with the spiritual renewal and with bringing people to the Lord - the very things the parish and diocese are concerned with. Our work is not additional to church life, it is central to it. We have a special way of doing it, but not more special than the Legion of Mary, for instance, or the Christian Family Movement. Our work in the Charismatic renewal should be accepted as work that supports the life and structures of the church.

### c) We should keep those in the Church who are over us informed of what is happening with us

Pastoral leadership cannot be exercised without information. If a pastor is not in contact with what is happening among the people he heads, he cannot be a very good pastor. This means that if we want to remain within the Catholic Church but not deal with its leaders, all we would have to do is "lie low". If we gave them little information and kept what we were doing out of view, we would be safe. But our goal is not to avoid the leaders we have, but rather to be in a good relationship with them. And we cannot say that we are in a good relationship with those who are over us in the Lord unless we submit our activities to them. (Heb. 13:17, I Th. 5:12-14, I Cor. 16:16).

We do not have to fear repressive or overly directive leadership from those in authority in the Catholic Church today. No leadership is perfect, and there have been times in the past when the leadership of the Church has been authoritarian. But today we need have little fear of that. Moreover, even if it were authoritarian, "lying low" would not be the right way to relate to it. The right approach now and always is to approach those who are over us with the trust that the Lord will watch over us and our relationship with them, and that he can take care of his work.

In general, the more we can communicate with bishops and pastors, the better. The more they know about the charismatic renewal and about our group, the better our relationship with them will be. The more they come to know that we will communicate openly with them the more readily they will trust us. This communication can take the following forms: a regular meeting with the bishop or pastor or with their representatives; regular reports; and personal contacts or letters from members of the diocese or parish to those who are over them. Whatever the means, the communication should be regular and open and it should involve some official contact.

**d) We should stay free of non-Catholic cultural baggage without neglecting to receive new things which are improvements in our old culture**

Our loyalty to the Church expressed in our support of its life is the main way in which we will be able to avoid division from other Catholics or from the Church as a whole. But in addition the way in which we approach the new thing we are concerned with - the charismatic dimension - will do a great deal to further or retard our unity with other Catholics. Because we are in contact with many Protestants, especially Evangelicals and Classical Pentecostals, it is easy for us to pick up what some have called "cultural baggage", that is, ways of expressing our life in the Spirit which are simply human customs that come from a different culture than our own.

Americans belong to a different culture than Polynesians. For Americans and Polynesians, Christianity is essentially the same (as is the life of the Spirit). But an American will express his life with Christ in ways that are determined by his being an American: he will sing hymns to an organ or a guitar and he will (often) wear a suit to religious services. If Polynesians are taught to sing songs to organs or guitars instead of to their native instruments, and are taught to wear suits to religious services when they are taught Christianity, they are being given Christianity plus cultural baggage.

It is not true that all cultures are equally good. Some cultures are deficient in certain respects compared with other cultures. Often when a people take over customs from other cultures, they are making an improvement in their own. It is therefore not always easy to tell when we are taking over cultural baggage or when we are making a cultural improvement. Worship through singing songs written in a folk idiom and spontaneous prayer were not part of American Catholic culture thirty years ago. Both are definite improvements in our Catholic culture. On the other hand sometimes Catholics start speaking King James English in religious contexts and start singing sentimental gospel songs because of their contacts with Classical Pentecostals. Both these things seem clear cases of taking over cultural baggage.

Even though it is difficult to discern in many cases how to apply it, the principle still holds true: the more our life in meetings of the charismatic renewal is expressed in our own culture as Catholics and in harmony with our tradition as Catholics the more we will be able to be at one with other Catholics who are not part of the charismatic renewal. We do not want to put up any unnecessary barriers to communication with them. We should try to form our life in the Spirit in such a way that we do not pick up cultural baggage, but yet do not lose new approaches that are of value and from God.

**15. To avoid division from Christians who do not belong to the Catholic Church, we should:**
   a) **sometimes form ecumenical groupings**
   b) **preserve brotherly communion with Christians involved in the charismatic renewal in other churches**
   c) **avoid making the uniquely Catholic the center of our focus**
   d) **avoid bring Catholic cultural baggage into ecumenical gatherings, and at the same time not fail to contribute good things from our Catholic culture which are improvements.**

Part of our concern as Christian leaders has to be an ecumenical concern, because it is the concern of the church today. But that ecumenical concern has to be worked out practically: we have to take steps to make it a reality. Moreover, those steps will be taken in a special way, because the charismatic renewal itself is an ecumenical movement and has always been so. Catholics who are involved in the charismatic renewal, simply because of that involvement, already find themselves in a relationship with certain other Christians. That relationship has provided a unique opportunity for "grass-roots ecumenism". Christians who have never before been able to talk with one another as Christians with any degree of unity find a genuine unity "in the Spirit". What is happening to us in this respect gives us a special responsibility for service in the church today and makes it important for the Lord's work that we understand the right practical steps to take and take them.

### a) We should sometimes form ecumenical groupings

If we are going to foster the unity of all Christians in the Spirit as we move forward in the charismatic renewal of the Catholic Church some of us ought to form ecumenical groupings that are charismatic. To be sure many of the groupings we form will be all-Catholic because in particular situations that will allow us to better reach the Catholic Church. My personal guess is that most Catholics who are involved in the charismatic renewal should be in Catholic groupings for some time to come for this will allow them more freedom and readiness to relate to their parish. But in many situations, the groupings we form should be ecumenical. Many of us will be called to live more fully now the unity which the whole Church is seeking.

There are many reasons for forming or becoming part of ecumenical groupings, most of them practical. Sometimes ecumenical groups are the only vital charismatic groups available to individual Catholics. At the moment however, it is more common to find groups started by Catholics that are attracting people who are not Catholics. There are groups like these all over the country which have grown out of the Catholic charismatic renewal and they are often the most vital charismatic groups available in their area. They are also the kind of groups which many Protestants find easier to relate to than more standard Pentecostal or "Full-Gospel" groups. People who are not Catholics want to be part of these groups for the sake of a deeper Christian life, and yet do not want to become Catholic. It is rarely right for us to turn them away. Consequently, that which we have come to call "the Catholic charismatic renewal" is probably made up of as many ecumenical groups as all-Catholic groups.

There is, however, a reason for forming ecumenical groups that is more than a matter of immediate practicality. If we are seriously committed to the unity of all Christians, we will want to move towards a serious committment of community (fellowship) and brotherhood with other Christians around us. While theologians and Church officials are working towards greater unity between church bodies, the members of churches should work towards greater unity with one another in a direct, person to person way. It is this movement toward unity around the gospel which is the most significant reason for forming ecumenical charismatic prayer groups communities and works of Christian service.

I have been talking here about "ecumenical groupings", not "interdenominational" groupings. By "interdenominational" groupings, I mean those who adopt the approach "it doesn't matter what church you belong to, as long as you are a Christian". In an interdenominational grouping whether you are a Catholic or not or whether you believe in Catholic teaching or not is irrelevant or at least should not be a matter of concern. As a matter of fact most "interdenominational" groups are conservative evangelical or fundamentalist in teaching and they effectively take the Catholics who are part of them away from being Catholics in any vital sense. By "ecumenical" groupings I mean those in which people's church membership and their commitment to their different churches and traditions is a matter of common concern. A Catholic's life as a Catholic is something which everyone in the group can come to understand and support, and he in turn can do that for those who are not Catholic. I have seen a much better understanding of Catholicism and a deeper commitment to the renewal of the Catholic Church among members of some ecumenical groups I have been part of than I have among most Catholic parishioners.

Essential to the formation of the right kind of ecumenical groupings is leadership which is able to help the group develop wisely. Often, however, Catholics get involved in groups that are under strong leadership of Classical Pentecostals (either in Pentecostal denominations or "independent"). Sometimes groups that are predominantly Catholic actually accept the leadership of Classical Pentecostals because they feel the need for "experienced" leadership. In such groups or under such leadership Catholics become less and less Catholic because the leaders do not understand Catholicism and, usually, do not sympathize with it. There will probably come a time when Classical Pentecostals will have undergone the kind of change which will make them genuinely open to Catholicism and able to participate in the leadership of genuinely ecumenical (and not just interdenominational) charismatic groupings. In the meantime, leadership for ecumenical groupings will probably only be found among Catholics and mainline Protestants. That is not to say that Catholics and mainline Protestants will automatically be able to be good leaders of an ecumenical group. Only when a person has an ecumenical commitment and an ecumenical sensitivity can he be a good leader of an ecumenical group.

b) **We should preserve a brotherly communion with Christians involved in the charismatic renewal in other churches**

Forming a Catholic charismatic renewal could isolate us from other Christians involved in the charismatic renewal, and in some situations it has. But it does not have to. Even when we do not form ecumenical prayer groups or communities, we can preserve a genuine communion with Christians of other Churches involved in the charismatic renewal, both as individual groups and as a movement. We can meet with them, invite them to our meetings, visit theirs, join with them in common projects, share literature with them, pray for them. And we should, to the degree that we can.

There are a variety of streams within the present charismatic renewal. One stream is represented by the Classical Pentecostals. A second is made up of people with an anti-denominational bias who urge people to stay clear of denominations and traditional churches. Most of those who are part of this second stream came out of Classical Pentecostal denominations. A third stream is represented by those who want to see their Churches renewed charismatically. We should have a genuine concern for all these streams including those who are in Classical Pentecostal denominations. (Many Catholics have neglected real contact with Pentecostal denominations and with people who are active members of them). But our primary concern at this moment in history should go to developing good relationships with those who are part of the charismatic renewal in other Churches.

Catholics and the Catholic charismatic renewal in general have been a significant influence in the last few years in strengthening the charismatic renewal in other Churches. The example of what is happening in the Catholic Church and the influence of individual Catholics and of predominantly Catholic prayer groups has led to the growth of charismatic renewal among Christians of many Churches. "If the

Catholics can do it, we can too!" However, not only has the example of the Catholic charismatic renewal been a stimulus; participants in the Catholic charismatic renewal have been able to be a direct help, with advice and other services, to the emerging charismatic movements in the other Churches. At the moment, this seems to be something that the Lord is bringing about and therefore something that should be a serious concern of ours.

### c) We should avoid making the uniquely Catholic the center of our focus

In order to maintain our ecumenical openness and our concern for communion with other Christians, we should also avoid making what is uniquely Catholic the center of our focus. By "uniquely Catholic" I mean such things as devotion to Mary and the saints, talking about "the sacraments" or the "sacramental system" (as distinguished from talking about baptism and the Eucharist), the parish structure and Catholic ecclesiastical politics, liturgical changes, and other similar things. Things which are not uniquely Catholic are God, Christ, the Holy Spirit, loving one another, avoiding sin, preaching the gospel, doing the works of mercy.

It is precisely those things which are not uniquely Catholic which, according to Catholic teaching, ought to occupy the center of our attention anyway. God himself and our relationship to him through Jesus should gain our fullest attention. Loving one another and serving other men should be second. Things which are uniquely Catholic have a place, but if we are going to be good Catholics they should not be the center of our attention.

The Sixteenth Century introduced a defensive attitude into the Catholic Church. Those things which we now see as uniquely Catholic were challenged, and in response Catholics defended them and focused on them to a degree that is unwarranted by their place in Catholic teaching. In recent years, especially through the Vatical Council, there has been a move toward restoring the perspective. And yet, many Catholics, especially when they get involved in ecumenical situations, who find themselves returning to the old defensiveness and wanting to refocus on and reemphasize the uniquely Catholic.

The uniquely Catholic has its place in our lives as Christians; it has a contribution to make to what the Lord is doing today. Without it, the fullness of Christianity is missing. We have no need to be ashamed of what is uniquely Catholic; do we need to be defensive about it? The Lord himself will defend it in his own wisdom. We should simply place the focus where the scriptures and the Church teach us that it ought to be.

**d) We should avoid bring Catholic cultural baggage into ecumenical gatherings, and at the same time not fail to contribute good things from our Catholic culture which are improvements.**

It goes without question that we should not bring that which is uniquely Catholic into gatherings that are ecumenical. If we expect Protestants to avoid saying "all you need is the Bible" (and we should expect them to), we should avoid praying to Mary. But we should also learn to be sensitive to Catholic cultural baggage. The same principle that leads us to avoid non-Catholic cultural baggage with Catholics should hold in the ecumenical area as well. In principle, there is no reason why devotion to the Sacred Heart should not be acceptable to Protestants (at least most forms of the devotion). But they do find it difficult to take, and there is no essential reason why we have to express our personal love to Jesus in this cultural form. On the other hand, there are improvements which we can offer which are cultural, but are nonetheless very helpful to Protestants. The songs which are current in the Catholic charismatic renewal are usually a definite improvement that non-Catholics can make use of. Liturgical worship is another (although it can be more touchy since it is so closely connected with the Catholic Eucharist). In short, we have to learn to be sensitive if we are going to avoid division from Christians who are not Catholics, but we do not have to be afraid to share many of the things the Lord has given us.

# FUTURE DEVELOPMENT

**16. We should be constantly looking to the Lord for his new directions.**

This is the third time I have re-written this set of guidelines. Each time I have rewritten them, I have made significant changes. The changes have come partly from my own growth and better understanding. But the changes have come mostly from the change in the situation. The Lord has moved on - what he is doing now is not exactly what he was doing two or five years ago. Guidelines which are appropriate in 1973 will be less appropriate in 1974 and still less appropriate in 1983.

In the book of Numbers (Ch. 9) it says, "so it was continually; the cloud covered the tent of the testimony by day and the appearance of fire by night. And whenever the cloud was taken up from over the tent, after that the people of Israel set out; and in the place where the cloud settled down, there the people of Israel encamped. At the command of the Lord the people of Israel set out, and at the command of the Lord they encamped; as long as the cloud rested over the tabernacle, they remained in camp. Even when the cloud continued over the tabernacle many days, the people of Israel kept the charge of the Lord and did not set out. Sometimes the cloud was a few days over the tabernacle, and according to the command of the Lord they remained in camp; then according to the command of the Lord they set out. And sometimes the cloud remained from evening until morning; and when the cloud was taken up in the morning, they set out, or if it continued for a day and a night, when the cloud was taken up they set out. Whether it was two days, or a month, or a longer time, that the cloud continued over the tabernacle, abiding there, the people of Israel remained in camp and did not set out; but when it was taken up they set out. At the command of the Lord they encamped, and at the command of the Lord they set out. They kept the charge of the Lord."

We must be like the people of Israel. When we perceive the presence of the Lord in something and see him at work, we should remain in that and serve there. When we see the presence lift and see him begin to work in new ways, we should follow him. Our task is to discern how the Lord is working and to be at the service of what he is doing. Our approach this year should not necessarily be our approach ten years from now.

I personally think that the charismatic renewal in the Catholic Church is going to turn out to be one of the most significant happenings in the whole history of the Church. We are seeing it spread rapidly and receive widespread acceptance. We are beginning to see it reach into many areas of Church life and lead to many changes. Because the charismatic renewal is so significant, and because the blessing of the Lord is so much upon it right now, we have to be all the more earnest to seek to discern what the Spirit is doing and to try to be servants of his work, following the direction he is setting.

Movements usually do not remain united for very long. The Pentecostal movement in its 70 years of existence has been noted for splintering and in-fighting (only something that was a real move of the Spirit could survive such a history). Often movements split because of ideology. Often they split because as different groups develop, they develop their own approach. Then these groups want more to work with others who have the same approach than they want to work with the movement as a whole. Moreover, as movements are accepted they tend to lose their cohesiveness.

Upholding something special against opposition (it turns out) was one of the main things keeping them together.

It is not bad that movements lose their special existence (who wants a special liturgical movement anymore?). But it should not happen before they perform their function in the life of the church. And preferably, they should not splinter and end up with different groups fighting one another. To avoid these things, the leaders of the movement must have wisdom, divine wisdom.

I am not sure how long there should be one recognizable movement for charismatic renewal in the Catholic Church. Certainly it should exist long enough for the life of the Spirit as we have experienced it and the spiritual gifts to be an accepted part of the life of the church. We do, however, need to recognize that we are in a second stage of charismatic renewal. Different approaches are developing. We need wisdom to know what forms groups involved in the charismatic renewal should take, how they should relate to the official structures of the church, how they should relate to ecumenical realities, how we should structure the international movement. Above all, our calling from God is to see that there is enough wisdom, brotherly love and attention to the leading of the Spirit that whatever development takes place will take place in unity of spirit, in a common concern for the glory of God and the life of the church, and in communion with one another.

"I pray for those who will believe in me.
May they all be one.

Rather, may they be one in us,
as you are in me and I in you,
so that the world may believe it was you who
sent me."

**TEAM MANUAL**
FOR THE LIFE IN THE SPIRIT SEMINARS
COMPLETELY REVISED
EDITED BY STEPHEN CLARK

Incorporating the experience of 4½ years, the Team Manual represents the experience and reflections of The Word of God, a Christian community in Ann Arbor, on leading people into baptism of the Holy Spirit, spiritual gifts and a full Christian life as members of a vital Christian community. The handbook format makes it ideal in leading people to yield fully to God's action in their lives.
**186 pp.**                                                    **$1.95**

**FINDING NEW LIFE IN THE SPIRIT**
This is the booklet recommended in the Life in the Spirit Team Manual. It supplements the Life in the Spirit seminars with daily readings and prayers to effectively prepare people to be baptized in the Spirit. Highly recommended reading for all those taking part in the Life in the Spirit seminars.
**46 pp.**                                                     **$.60**

**THE LIFE IN THE SPIRIT SEMINARS**
BY THE WORD OF GOD, ANN ARBOR, MICHIGAN
Contains explanation session and seminars No. 1-7
**LSB 1,2,3,4 (4 Cassettes)**                    **$15.00**

**THE LIFE IN THE SPIRIT SEMINARS – TEACHING AND DYNAMICS**
BERT GHEZZI – DOUG GAVRILIDES
Two talks which are necessary for understanding the use of the seminars. Discusses: Vision behind the new LSS outlines; how to make them work well; the need to adapt the seminars to various local situations; the dynamics of the presentations; building up the team; how to deal with particular needs of people.
**A-1071 (C-90 Cassette)**                        **$4.50**

## HELPING PEOPLE APPROPRIATE GOD'S LIFE
BERT GHEZZI

The role of the discussion leaders in Life in the Spirit Seminars and Foundations Courses involves more than keeping a discussion going — they are helping people come into a new life in the Holy Spirit. This talk defines that role and gives practical advice on how to fill it.

A-1084                                                              $3.95

## THE LORD, THE SPIRIT AND THE CHURCH
KEVIN RANAGHAN

This booklet outlines how charismatic Catholics can freely rejoice in what the Lord is doing throughout his whole Body, and yet recognize that the charismatic renewal is a tool from the Lord specifically for the spiritual renewal of the Catholic Church. A powerfully inspirational and practical teaching by the co-author of **Catholic Pentecostals** and co-editor of **As The Spirit Leads Us.**

$.75

## GROWING IN FAITH
STEPHEN CLARK

Have you been recently baptized in the Spirit? Or have you been living the Christian life for some time now? Do you need direction to grow in faith? Steve Clark offers clear and practical guidance on how to take deeper steps in faith in Jesus.

**64 pp.**                                                          **$.60**

### DISCOUNT SCHEDULE
10% on $15.00 orders
15% on $25.00 orders
20% on $50.00 orders

### ORDER BOTH BOOKS AND
### CASSETTES FROM:

Charismatic Renewal Services
Communication Center
P.O. Drawer A
Notre Dame, Indiana 46556